I love reading

Prehistoric Swimming Giants

by Monica Hughes

Consultant: Dougal Dixon

CONTENTS

Words in **bold** are explained in the glossary.

Swimming creatures

There were **prehistoric** creatures in the seas at the time of the dinosaurs.

Some were big. Some were small.

Ceresiosaurus
ser-ee-see-o-sor-us

Many had sharp teeth to
catch fish.

Placodus

This is Placodus. It was about two metres long.

It had four legs and **webbed feet.**

Webbed feet

Newt

It looked like a giant newt.

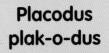

Placodus
plak-o-dus

A giant sea creature

This swimming giant was 15 metres long.

It had a long head and sharp teeth.

Kronosaurus
kroh-no-sor-us

It ate octopus and giant **squid**.

What a long neck!

This swimming creature was very big.

Its neck was longer than its body.

Elasmosaurus
ee-las-mo-sor-us

It had a short tail.

It had legs like **paddles**.

On land and in the sea

This creature went on land,
but mostly it lived in the sea.

Nothosaurus
noth-o-sor-us

It had webbed feet
to help it to swim.

Snake or turtle?

This creature had a long neck and sharp teeth.

Fish

It ate fish and squid.

It looked like **a cross**
between a snake and
a turtle.

Cryptoclidus
crip-tow-cly-dus

Fish-lizard

This swimming creature was as big as a dolphin.

Its name means 'fish-lizard'.

Ichthyosaurus
ick-thee-o-sor-us

Squid

It ate fish and squid.

A huge sea monster

Look at Shonisaurus.
This creature was as big as a whale.

Whale

It could swim in deep water.

It ate fish and other sea creatures.

Shonisaurus
show-ni-sor-rus

19

What a long creature!

This creature had a long body
and a flat tail.

It had a long nose and sharp teeth.

Tylosaurus
tie-low-sor-us

It had legs like paddles.

Glossary

a cross
Partly one thing and partly another.

paddles
Flat blades that push through water.

prehistoric
The millions of years before human history.

squid
A boneless sea creature with tentacles.

webbed feet
When toes are joined together by skin.

Index

Copyright © ticktock Entertainment Ltd 2008
First published in Great Britain in 2008 by ticktock Media Ltd.,
Unit 2, Orchard Business Centre, North Farm Road, Tunbridge Wells, Kent TN2 3XF
ISBN 978 1 84696 754 2 pbk
Printed in China

We would like to thank: Penny Worms, Shirley Bickler, Suzanne Baker, and the National Literacy Trust.

Picture credits (t=top, b=bottom, c=centre, l-left, r=right, OFC= outside front cover)
John Alston: 5b; Simon Mendez: 1, 4-5, 8-9, 12-13, 19, 20-21, 23t, 23b; Luis Rey: 1, 6, 14-15, 16-17, 22t; Shutterstock: 7t, 8, 10-11, 14, 17t, 18, 23b, 23c.